Editor
Lorin E. Klistoff, M.A.

Editor in Chief
Ina Massler Levin, M.A.

Illustrator
Renée Christine Yates

Cover Artist
Courtney Barnes

Creative Director
Karen J. Goldfluss, M.S. Ed.

Art Production Manager
Kevin Barnes

Art Coordinator
Renée Christine Yates

Imaging
Craig Gunnell

Publisher
Mary D. Smith, M.S. Ed.

Author

Penny Carter

Teacher Created Resources, Inc.
6421 Industry Way
Westminster, CA 92683
www.teachercreated.com

ISBN: 978-1-4206-8976-1

© 2008 Teacher Created Resources, Inc.
Made in U.S.A.

Table of Contents

Introduction

Using poetry with children is a wonderful way to instruct and motivate. In this book, *Phonics Poetry Using Digraphs*, consonant digraphs are presented in poems which repeatedly use a particular digraph sound. Children are also given opportunities to practice the sounds through the use of reproducible activity pages involving both reading and writing activities. These poems and activity pages can be presented in different ways depending on the age and ability level of the children. For younger children, the poems can be read together as a class. The teacher can guide the children through the process of listening for and locating the digraphs. Older children can utilize the sounds to decipher words on their own.

Before each new digraph sound is presented, prepare a copy of the appropriate poem for each child. Read through the poem first and carry on a discussion to make sure the children comprehend the message of the poem. Then reread, or have the children reread, and highlight the words containing the digraph sound. Some of the activity pages are suitable for the younger primary child, while others are geared toward upper primary.

You might want to let the students take the poems home to practice, or you might prefer that the students save their poems to become part of a poetry collection.

We hope that you and your students enjoy using these poems and worksheets. We feel certain that they will help to provide engaging and effective phonics practice in your integrated reading and writing program.

CORRELATION OF STANDARDS

Standard: Uses the general skills and strategies of the reading process

- Creates mental images from pictures and print

- Uses basic elements of phonetic analysis to decode unknown words

- Reads aloud familiar stories, poems, and passages with fluency and expression

Standard: Uses reading skills and strategies to understand and interpret a variety of literary texts

- Uses reading skills and strategies to understand a variety of familiar literary passages and texts (e.g., poems)

Standard: Uses listening and speaking strategies for different purposes

- Recites and responds to familiar stories, poems, and rhymes with patterns

*All standards listed above are from *A Compendium of Standards and Benchmarks for K–12 Education* (Copyright 2004 McREL, www.mcrel.org/standards-benchmarks) Language Arts (Grades K–2).

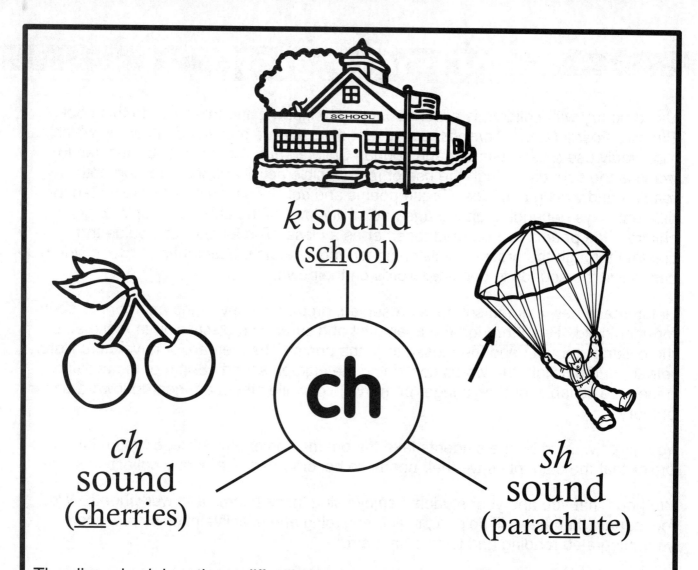

k sound
(s<u>ch</u>ool)

ch
sound
(<u>ch</u>erries)

ch

sh
sound
(para<u>ch</u>ute)

The digraph *ch* has three different sounds. The most common of the three is the sound found at the beginning of the word <u>cherry</u>. When children are trying to decipher a word which has a *ch* in it, they should be taught to try this sound first. If the word does not make sense using this sound, the second sound, or the sound of *k* such as in the word *school*, should be tried. The third sound of *ch* is the *sh* sound, as in the word *para<u>ch</u>ute*. This sound should be tried last since it is not used in our English language as frequently.

Children need practice reading words that have the digraph sound at the beginning, middle, and end of a word. Children should be taught that when *ch* is located at the end of a word, it is often preceded by a *t*. Examples are the words *watch* and *witch*; the exception is the word *lunch*.

This section contains poems and activity pages that provide reading and writing practice using all three sounds of *ch* in various placements. To practice the *ch* sound as in *cherry*, use the two poems, "Chicken Pox" and "My Dog, Charlie." The poem "The Character Show" utilizes the *k* sound of *ch*. The poem "Parachuting Cher" deals with the *sh* sound of *ch*. The last of the *ch* poems combines all three sounds in a poem called "Charlotte's Trip."

Chicken Pox

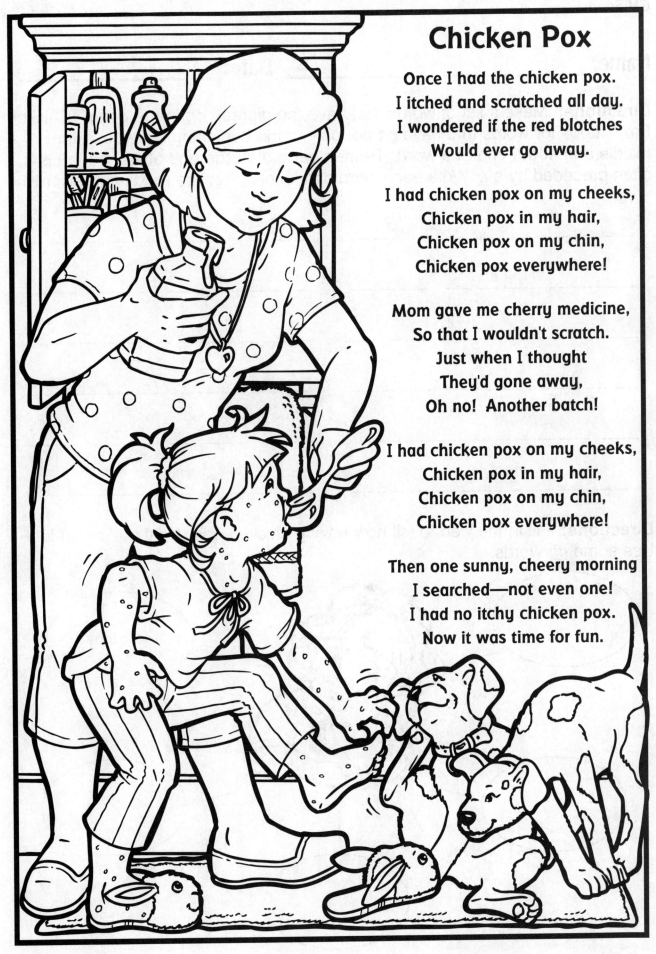

Once I had the chicken pox.
I itched and scratched all day.
I wondered if the red blotches
Would ever go away.

I had chicken pox on my cheeks,
Chicken pox in my hair,
Chicken pox on my chin,
Chicken pox everywhere!

Mom gave me cherry medicine,
So that I wouldn't scratch.
Just when I thought
They'd gone away,
Oh no! Another batch!

I had chicken pox on my cheeks,
Chicken pox in my hair,
Chicken pox on my chin,
Chicken pox everywhere!

Then one sunny, cheery morning
I searched—not even one!
I had no itchy chicken pox.
Now it was time for fun.

#8976 Phonics Poetry Using Digraphs

Name: _____ **Date:** _____

Directions: Make a list of words that have the digraph *ch* in the poem "Chicken Pox." Look for words that have *ch* not only at the beginning but also in the middle and at the end of a word. Remember that at the end of a word, *ch* is often preceded by a *t*. Write each word only once. Practice reading the words.

_____   _____

_____   _____

_____   _____

_____   _____

_____   _____

_____   _____

Directions: Fill in the web to tell how having chicken pox might make you feel. Use some *ch* words.

scratchy

Name: _____ **Date:** _____

Directions: Read the story below. Fill in the blanks with a word that has a *ch* digraph in it. Choose the words from the word box that make sense in the sentences.

su<u>ch</u>	**wat<u>ch</u>ed**	**<u>ch</u>at**
<u>ch</u>air	**<u>ch</u>ocolate**	**<u>ch</u>icken**

Once I had the _____ pox and couldn't

1

go anywhere. The days went by slowly. I just sat in a

_____ and _____ T.V. for hours. Then one

2   3

day Mom came home with a box of _____ candy.

4

She sat with me, and we had a _____. That was

5

_____ a lovely treat. Being sick wasn't so bad after all!

6

Directions: If you had the chicken pox and couldn't go out to play, what are some things that you could do to make the day go faster?

1. _____

_____

2. _____

_____

My Dog, Charlie

My dog, Charlie, likes to chew
A chair, the sofa, and my shoe.

When outside, he chews some more—
Branches, his chain, and our back door.

He searches high; he searches low.
He chews a sock; he chews my toe.

But give him dog food for his lunch,
Not a nibble, not a crunch.

He chooses just to walk away.
"Such a naughty dog," I say.

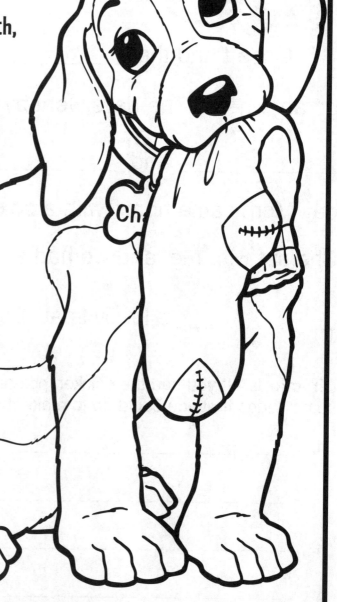

Name: _____ **Date:** _____

Directions: The poem, "My Dog, Charlie" makes use of the most common sound of <u>ch</u>. Make a list of the words containing a <u>ch</u> digraph found in this poem. Use each word only once. Practice reading the words.

_____   _____

_____   _____

_____   _____

_____   _____

Directions: Fill in the web to tell what things in the poem Charlie should not have chewed.

a chair

Name: _____ **Date:** _____

Directions: Read the story below. Fill in the blanks with a word that has a *ch* digraph in it. Choose the words from the word box that make sense in the sentences.

Charlie

chew	lunch	choke
cherry	cheese	chicken

I tried to get Charlie to eat his dog food for _____ .
                                                                    1
He just didn't want to eat it. Then I had an idea! If I put

_____ sauce all over his food, maybe he would eat
          2
it. I even put a _____ on top. He still wouldn't even
                          3
come near it. Next, I mixed his food with some bits of

_____ . That did the trick! Charlie ate so fast that he
          4
started to _____ . I laughed and said, "Charlie,
                      5
_____ a little slower."
          6

Directions: What is something else that you might add to Charlie's lunch to get him to eat it?

_____

_____

_____

Name: _____ **Date:** _____

Directions: We all know that dogs love to chew bones. If Charlie only chews the bones with the _ch_ sound, tell which of the following he would chew. Write *Yes* or *No* in the blanks.

1.  _____

2.  _____

3. 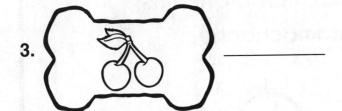 _____

4.  _____

5.  _____

6. 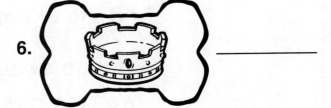 _____

7. 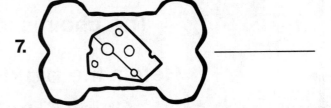 _____

8.  _____

9. 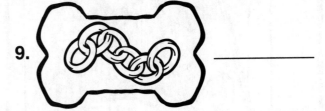 _____

10.  _____

The Character Show

At school we're having a character show,
And I can hardly wait.
Chris' character is Johnny Chrome,
And the chemist will be Kate.

I dance away in the chorus.
We sing a wonderful song.
The voices echo off the walls.
The choir is loud and strong!

Here's the big day; are we ready?
Oh no! My leg did break.
Poor Chris, he's sick with bronchitis.
Kate has a stomachache.

Name: _____ **Date:** _____

Directions: Make a list of words from the poem, "The Character Show," that have the <u>k</u> sound of <u>ch</u>. Make an "X" in the column—whether you hear the sound at the **B** (beginning), **M** (middle), or **E** (end) of the word.

	B	**M**	**E**
school		X	

Name: _____ **Date:** _____

Directions: Pretend that your school is putting on a show. Make a list telling who some of the characters in your show might be.

_____

_____

_____

_____

_____

_____

_____

Directions: Tell about a time that you were planning to do something special and never got to do it. Why didn't you do it?

_____

_____

_____

_____

_____

Parachuting Cher

Cher parachuted from a plane
In Chicago one cold day.
The brochure called it, "The Windy City."
That's why she blew away.

She landed on a huge machine.
Then down a chute she slid.
She said, "Next time,
I'll blow through in my Chevy."
And that is what she did.

Name: _____ **Date:** _____

Directions: Color the parachutes where <u>ch</u> makes the <u>sh</u> sound as in *chef*.

1.
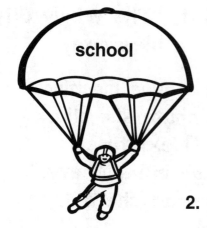
school

3.

chiffon

2.

chute

4.

Chicago

5.

church

7.

chandelier

6.

cheer

8.

machine

Name: _____ **Date:** _____

Directions: Make a list of words from the poem, "Parachuting Cher," that make the *sh* sound for the digraph *ch*. Mark an "X" in the correct column—whether you hear the sound at the **B** (beginning), **M** (middle), or **E** (end) of the word.

	B	**M**	**E**
Cher	X		

Directions: Pretend that Cher could only land in places where the *ch* digraph makes the *sh* sound. Write *yes* or *no* to tell where Cher could land.

1. at a school ————

2. in Chicago ————

3. in Charlotte ————

4. in Cherry Hill ————

5. in Cheyenne ————

6. at a church ————

Name: _____   **Date:** _____

Charlotte's Trip

Charlotte went to Chicago.
A school bus took her there.
She packed herself a picnic lunch—
Some chicken and a pear.

Charlotte visited her friends—
Chad, Chris, and Chucky, too.
She brought them all peach pie
And cherry gum to chew!

Directions: Write the words from the poem that have the *ch* digraph. Put them under the correct sound (*ch*, *k*, or *sh*).

ch	k	sh

shoes

sh

Children can easily remember the sound of *sh*
when it is referred to as the "teacher" sound.
Teachers very often make this sound when
they put a finger on their lips to indicate that
they want someone to be quiet. Practice the *sh*
sound through the use of the poems "Shelly's
Shoes" and "Fireman Joe's Galoshes."

Shelly's Shoes

Shelly wore her shiny shoes
When she went to the show.
Her shiny shoes got dirty.
It was the rodeo.

Shelly had no shiny shoes.
Oh my! What should she do?
Shelly's mom did shriek and shout,
"Oh Shelly, shame on you!"

Shelly got some polish out.
She got her dad's old shirt.
She rubbed the shoes until they shone,
And you could see no dirt!

20

Name: _____ **Date:** _____

Directions: Make a list of the words containing the *sh* digraph found in the poem, "Shelly's Shoes." Circle the word that has *sh* at the end. Practice reading the words.

_____   _____

_____   _____

_____   _____

_____   _____

_____   _____

Directions: Shelly wore her shiny shoes to a rodeo, and they got very dirty. Circle the places in the list below to tell where you should <u>NOT</u> wear shiny shoes.

I should not wear shiny shoes when I go to . . .

a baseball game   the playground

a wedding   gym class

a church   the circus

Name: _____ **Date:** _____

Directions: Tell whether the following are examples of things that are shiny or not shiny. Write *yes* if they are shiny. Write *no* if they are not shiny.

1. new shoes _____ **2.** diamond ring _____

3. tennis shoes _____ **4.** flower _____

5. cake _____ **6.** new car _____

7. cat _____ **8.** bed _____

9. star in the sky _____ **10.** new coin _____

Directions: Write a few sentences about something shiny. Try to include as many <u>sh</u> words as you can.

_____

_____

_____

_____

_____

Fireman Joe's Galoshes

Fireman Joe wears galoshes.
He polishes them each day.
And when the fire whistle shrieks,
He hurries right away.

On go his big galoshes.
He does it in a flash.
And in a very short time,
The truck begins to dash.

Soon a puddle starts to form
When Joe gets out his hose.
There's no time for foolishness,
Shh, Shh, the water goes.

Fireman Joe's galoshes
Run with him here and there.
He splishes and he splashes,
Until there's fire nowhere!

Name: _____ **Date:** _____

Directions: Make a list of the words containing the digraph <u>sh</u> found in the poem, "Fireman Joe's Galoshes." Write each word only once. Practice reading the words.

_____   _____

_____   _____

_____   _____

_____   _____

_____   _____

Directions: Draw a picture of yourself wearing galoshes. Fireman Joe fights fires in his galoshes. What could you do in yours? Show this in your picture. Then write a sentence to explain your picture.

_____

_____

Name: _____ **Date:** _____

Directions: The poem, "Fireman Joe's Galoshes," uses special words to describe sounds.

1. What words describe the sounds that Joe's galoshes make?

   _____   _____

2. What sound is made by the water coming out of Joe's hose?

   _____

3. What word describes the sound made by the fire whistle?

   _____

Directions: Draw and describe something that might make the following sound: CRASH.

_____

_____

_____

f sound
(<u>ph</u>one)

ph

The *ph* digraph found in a word makes the sound of the letter *f*. Practice the sound through the use of the poems "The Telephone Itch" and "Funny Photos."

The Telephone Itch

When I'm near a telephone,
I have to make a call.
It doesn't matter who I dial,
Sophie, Ralph, or Paul.

Today I called my nephew,
Although he wasn't there.
I talked and talked just the same,
And gosh, I didn't care.

I think I have a sickness,
A telephone disease.
I'll call up my physician,
And we can shoot the breeze.

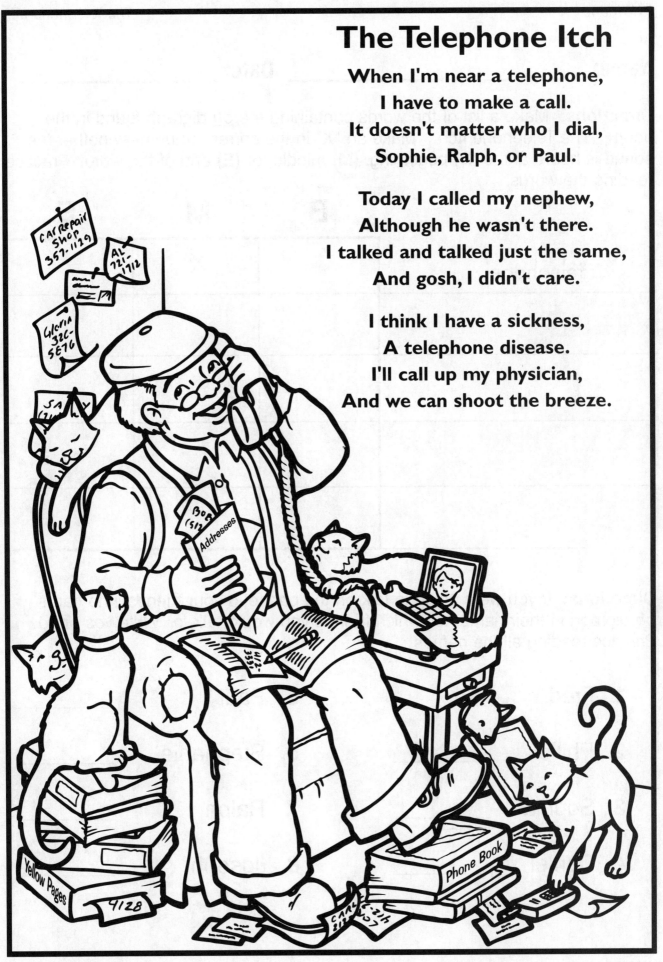

Name: _____ **Date:** _____

Directions: Make a list of the words containing the *ph* digraph found in the poem, "The Telephone Itch." Make an "X" in the correct column—whether the sound is heard at the (**B**) beginning, (**M**) middle, or (**E**) end of the word. Practice reading the words.

	B	M	E
telephone		X	

Directions: If you were going to talk on the phone to your friends who had a *ph* digraph in their name, tell which friends you would talk to. Write *yes* or *no*. Practice reading all the names.

1. Fred _____   **5.** Paul _____

2. Philip _____   **6.** Stephanie _____

3. Sophia _____   **7.** Ralph _____

4. Daniel _____   **8.** Joseph _____

Name: _____ **Date:** _____

Directions: Pretend you are talking on the telephone. Write what you might say to each person below. Include some *ph* words in your writing.

1. Your friend Ral<u>ph</u>

_____

_____

_____

2. Your <u>ph</u>ysician

_____

_____

_____

3. An ele<u>ph</u>ant at the zoo

_____

_____

_____

Funny Photos

Phillip took a photograph
Of a happy pheasant.
But when he got the photo back,
The pheasant wasn't pleasant.

Phillip took a photograph
Of an elephant in the zoo.
But when he got the photo back,
The elephant seemed blue.

Phillip took a photograph
Of his sweet dog, Josephine.
But when he got the photo back,
Sweet Josephine looked mean.

Phillip couldn't understand,
Each smile was a frown.
"Aha!" he said, "I think I know;
My camera's upside down."

Name: _____ **Date:** _____

Directions: Make a list of words that have the digraph _ph_ in the poem, "Funny Photos." Check the space that tells where you hear the _ph_ digraph sound— **B** for beginning, **M** for middle, or **E** for ending. Practice reading the words.

	B	M	E
Phillip	X		

Directions: Draw a picture of the dog, Josephine, from the poem. Show what she looked like *before* the photo and *in* the photo.

Before the photo	**In the photo**

Name: _____ **Date:** _____

Directions: Read the story below. Fill in the blanks with a word that has a *ph* digraph in it. Choose the words from the word box that make sense in the sentences.

dol<u>ph</u>ins	**pam<u>ph</u>lets**	**Philadel<u>ph</u>ia**
<u>Ph</u>illies	**ele<u>ph</u>ant**	**<u>ph</u>oto**

The city of _____ is a very famous city. At the zoo,

1

you can see large animals, such as an _____ , or you

2

can watch the _____ swim. You can visit the Liberty

3

Bell and buy a _____ of it. You can read historical

4

_____ at Independence Hall. What I like best about

5

this city is going to watch my favorite baseball team play—Go

_____ , go!

6

whale

wh

Wh is the digraph that begins many words that ask a question, such as *where, when, why,* and *what.* Occasionally, the *wh* digraph also makes the sound of *h* as in the words *who* and *whole.* Since this sound of *wh* is not as common, the poems in this book only deal with the *w* sound. Practice the *wh* sound through the use of the poems "Little White Whale" and "Questions."

Little White Whale

Little white whale
Where is your home?
Down in the ocean
Where there's room to roam.

Little white whale
What do you do?
I swim, I whistle,
And I play like you.

Little white whale
Why do you jump?
I take in some air
While my tail, I thump.

Little white whale
When do you sleep?
Whenever I want
In the water deep.

Name: _____ **Date:** _____

Directions: Make a list of <u>wh</u> words from the poem, "Little White Whale," that ask a question.

_____   _____

_____   _____

Directions: Make a list of <u>wh</u> words from the poem, "Little White Whale," that are not question words.

_____   _____

_____   _____

_____

Directions: Write a question using one of the question words above.

_____

_____

_____

Directions: If you could ask the little white whale a question, what would it be?

_____

_____

_____

Name: _____ **Date:** _____

Directions: Read the story below. Fill in the blanks with a word that has a *wh* digraph in it. Choose the words from the word box that make sense in the sentence.

WORD BOX				
which	whip	whistle	whale	white
what	when	whine	whiff	

You need lots of patience for _____ watching.

1

Do not _____ if it takes a long time to see a whale.

2

_____ you do spot one, it will be worth the wait. The

3

first thing you will probably notice is the blow or spout. This is a

puff of air _____ is exhaled through the blowhole. If

4

you see a beluga whale, it might be gray. Beluga whales turn

_____ as they grow older. The beluga whale is very

5

friendly and curious. Sometimes it makes a deep dive, and you

can see it _____ its tail in the air. Sometimes it leaps

6

out of the water as if it were a jack-in-the-box. _____

7

a sight that is to see! If you listen closely, you might hear the

whale _____ . I can't wait to get a _____ of

8   9

that ocean air and go whale watching once again.

Questions

My mother says
I drive her nuts!
Asking questions—
Where, Why, What's?

What's for dinner?
When will we eat?
Why potatoes?
Which kind of meat?

Where are we going?
Can't Duke come, too?
When will we get there?
What will I do?

Why is it bedtime?
Why can't I play?
Why did I get
In trouble today?

Name: _____ **Date:** _____

Directions: Pretend that you are on a shopping trip for a new pair of tennis shoes. Fill in the blanks with a <u>wh</u> question word that makes sense in each sentence. You can use the same word more than once.

WORD BOX
When   What   Where   Why   Which

1. _____ is the shoe store?

2. _____ will we get to the store?

3. _____ one of these stores sells shoes?

4. I like my old shoes. _____ do I need new shoes?

5. _____ will they look like?

6. _____ of these shoes do you like?

7. _____ is that color called?

8. _____ do I have to get white shoes?

9. _____ can't I wear them home?

10. _____ will they stop hurting my feet?

Name: _____ **Date:** _____

Directions: Many question words begin with the _wh_ digraph. Pretend you are traveling in a car with your parents, and the trip is taking a long time. What are some questions you might ask your parents? Use the _wh_ question words provided.

1. **When**

   _____

   _____

2. **What**

   _____

   _____

3. **Where**

   _____

   _____

4. **Why**

   _____

   _____

5. **Which**

   _____

   _____

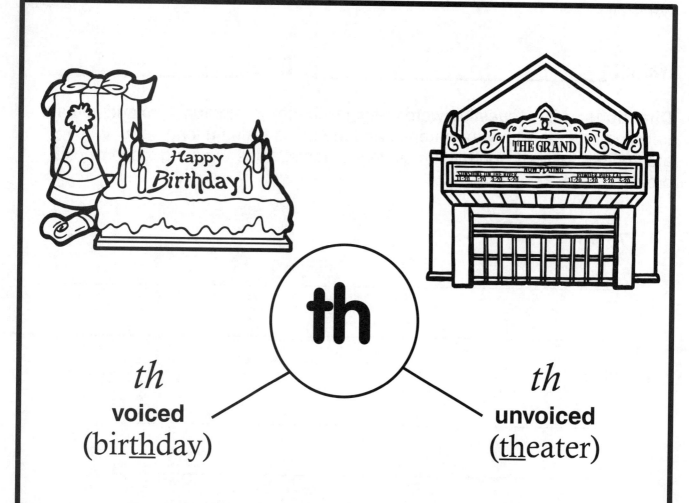

<table>
<tr><td>th
voiced
(bir<u>th</u>day)</td><td></td><td>th
unvoiced
(<u>th</u>eater)</td></tr>
</table>

The *th* digraph has a voiced and unvoiced sound. The amount of movement of the vocal cords determines which sound is heard. To find out if the *th* is voiced, place three fingers over your throat and say the word containing *th*. If you feel vibrations, the *th* is voiced. If you do not feel vibrations, it is unvoiced. A good example of a voiced *th* is the word *thee*. A good example of an unvoiced *th* is *thin*. Practice the *th* sound through the use of the poems "Birthday Wish" and "The Theater."

Birthday Wish

When my birthday comes this month,
I'll list the things I'd like.
I think that this could be the year
I'll get that brand new bike.

I told my mother if I did,
That I'd be good as gold.
I'd remember "please" and "thank you."
The laundry I'd help fold.

But if I didn't get that bike,
She wouldn't know what to do.
For I would simply hold my breath
And thoroughly turn blue.

Name: _____ Date: _____

Directions: Make a list of words from the poem, "Birthday Wish," that have the *th* sound. Write each word only once. Mark whether you hear the sound at the **B** (beginning), **M** (middle), or **E** (end) of the word. Practice reading the words.

	B	M	E
birthday		X	

Directions: Write your answer to the following:

Holding your breath is not a good thing to do. What is another way you might convince your mother to get you a new bike for your birthday?

Name: _____ **Date:** _____

Directions: Read the story below. Fill in the blanks with a word that has a *th* digraph in it. Choose the words from the word box that make sense in the sentences.

```
┌─────────────────────────────────────────────────┐
│                   WORD BOX                        │
│   mother         birthday         things          │
│   thank          month            think           │
└─────────────────────────────────────────────────┘
```

I am happy it is the _____ of June. Soon it will
                          1

be my sixth _____ . I'm sure I will get lots of new
                  2

_____ to play with. My _____ might
        3   4

buy me a new dress. I will say _____ you for all my
                                        5

gifts. I _____ it's going to be the best day ever!
                6

Directions: Write your answer to the following: What are some gifts you would like to get on your birthday?

_____

_____

_____

_____

Name: _____ **Date:** _____

Directions: Which of the following words, containing the *th* digraph, would make good gifts? Write *yes* or *no*.

1. a ba<u>th</u>tub _____

6. a <u>th</u>umbtack _____

2. a ma<u>th</u> book _____

7. <u>th</u>eater tickets _____

3. a <u>th</u>ousand dollars _____

8. a too<u>th</u>brush _____

4. a <u>th</u>ermometer _____

9. a new baby bro<u>th</u>er _____

5. a <u>th</u>oroughbred horse _____

10. a <u>th</u>imble _____

Directions: Circle the one you think would be the best birthday gift and tell why.

_____

_____

_____

_____

_____

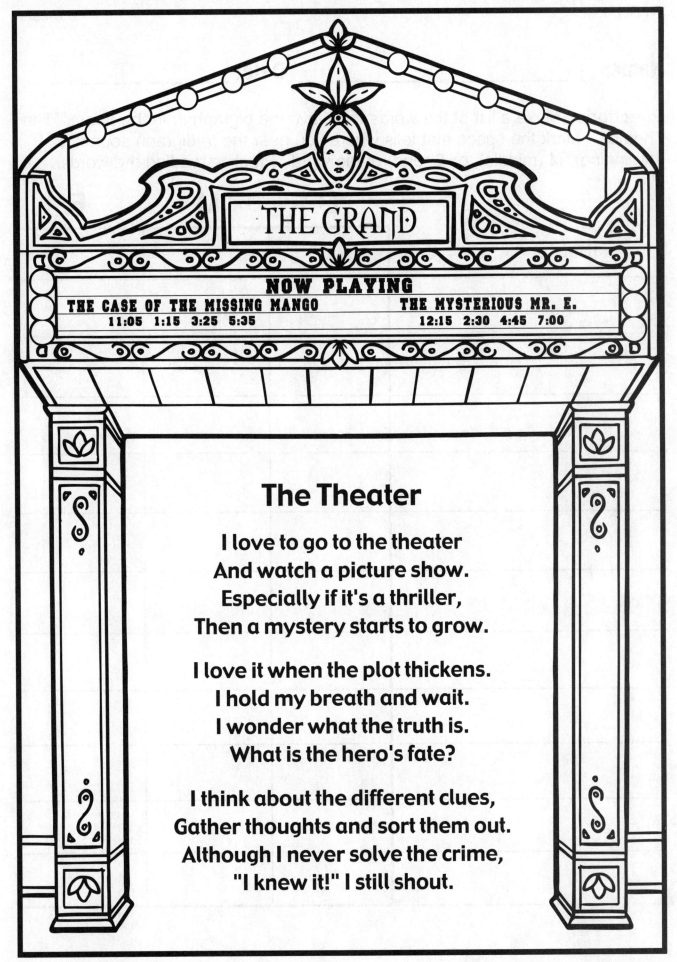

THE GRAND

NOW PLAYING

THE CASE OF THE MISSING MANGO
11:05 1:15 3:25 5:35

THE MYSTERIOUS MR. E.
12:15 2:30 4:45 7:00

The Theater

I love to go to the theater
And watch a picture show.
Especially if it's a thriller,
Then a mystery starts to grow.

I love it when the plot thickens.
I hold my breath and wait.
I wonder what the truth is.
What is the hero's fate?

I think about the different clues,
Gather thoughts and sort them out.
Although I never solve the crime,
"I knew it!" I still shout.

Name: _____ **Date:** _____

Directions: Make a list of the words that have the digraph *th* in the poem, "The Theater." Mark the space that tells where you hear the *th* digraph sound: **B** (beginning), **M** (middle), or **E** (end) of the word. Practice reading the words.

	B	M	E
theater	X		

Name: _____ **Date:** _____

Directions: Listed below are some titles of make-believe movies. Fill in the missing words with a word from the word box containing a *th* digraph.

WORD BOX
Thoroughbred   **Earth**   **Throne**   **Youth**   **Thunder**

1. _____ and Lightning

2. Finding the Fountain of _____

3. The _____ Horse

4. The King's Magic _____

5. My Life on Planet _____

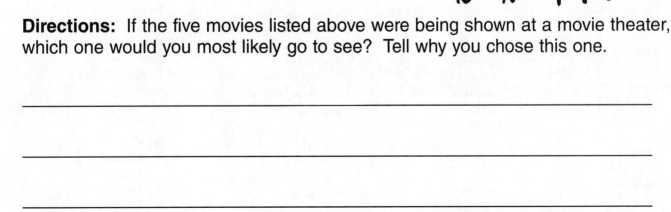

Directions: If the five movies listed above were being shown at a movie theater, which one would you most likely go to see? Tell why you chose this one.

_____

_____

_____

_____

Answer Key

Page 6

chicken	cherry
itched	scratch
scratched	batch
blotches	cheery
cheeks	searched
chin	itchy

Possible answers for the web are as follows: *itchy, angry, bored, ugly, frustrated, splotchy, blotchy*

Page 7

1. chicken 4. chocolate
2. chair   5. chat
3. watched 6. such

Possible answers for the question are as follows: watch TV, read a book, play games, write a letter

Page 9

Charlie	searches
chew(s)	lunch
chair	crunch
branches	chooses
chain	such

Possible answers for the web: a sofa, a shoe, the back door, a toe (Branches and his chain can also be accepted.)

Page 10

1. lunch   4. chicken
2. cheese 5. choke
3. cherry 6. chew

Possible answers for the question might include any types of meat products or snack foods.

Page 11

1. yes   6. no
2. no   7. yes
3. yes   8. no
4. no   9. yes
5. no   10. yes

Page 13

school–M
character–B
Chris–B
Chrome–B
chemist–B
chorus–B
echo–M
choir–B
bronchitis–M
stomachache–M/E

Page 14

Answers will vary.

Page 16

Numbers 2, 3, 4, 7 and 8 should be colored.

Page 17

Cher–B
parachuted–M
Chicago–B
brochure–M
machine–M
chute–B
Chevy–B

1. no   4. no
2. yes   5. yes
3. yes   6. no

Page 18

CH–lunch, chicken, Chad, Chucky, peach, cherry, chew
K–school, Chris
SH–Charlotte, Chicago

Page 21

Shelly	shriek
shiny	shout
shoes	shame
show	polish
should	shirt
she	shone

Polish should be circled. The following should be circled: a baseball game, the playground, gym class, the circus.

Page 22

1. yes   6. yes
2. yes   7. no
3. no   8. no
4. no   9. yes
5. no   10. yes

Answers will vary.

Page 24

galoshes
polishes
shrieks
flash
short
dash
foolishness
shh
splishes
splashes

The picture and sentence should describe something done while wearing galoshes, such as playing in the rain or shoveling snow.

Page 25

1. splishes, splashes
2. shh
3. shrieks

Possible answers: something breaking, thunder, or cars colliding

Page 28

telephone–M
Sophie–M
Ralph–E
nephew–M
physician–B

1. no   5. no
2. yes   6. yes
3. yes   7. yes
4. no   8. yes

Page 29

Answers will vary.

Page 31

Phillip–B
photograph–B/E
pheasant–B
photo–B
elephant–M
Josephine–M

"Before the photo" should show a sweet-looking dog. "In the photo" should show a mean-looking dog.

Page 32

1. Philadelphia 4. photo
2. elephant   5. pamphlets
3. dolphins   6. Phillies

Page 35

Question words: *where, what, why, when*
Not question words: *white, whale, whistle, while, whenever*
Answers to the last two questions will vary.

Page 36

1. whale   6. whip
2. whine   7. What
3. When   8. whistle
4. which   9. whiff
5. white

Page 38

1. Where   6. Which
2. When   7. What
3. Which   8. Why
4. Why   9. Why
5. What   10. When

Page 39

Answers will vary.

Page 42

birthday–M
month–E
the–B
things–B
think–B
that–B
this–B
mother–M
thank–B
breath–E
thoroughly–B

Answers to question will vary.

Page 43

1. month   4. mother
2. birthday 5. thank
3. things   6. think

Answers to question will vary.

Page 44

1. no   6. no
2. no   7. yes
3. yes   8. no
4. no   9. yes
5. yes   10. no

Answers may vary. They will reflect the students' opinions. Students should justify their choice.

Page 46

theater–B
thriller–B
then–B
thickens–B
breath–E
truth–E
think–B
gather–M
thoughts–B
them–B
although–M
the–B

Page 47

1. Thunder
2. Youth
3. Thoroughbred
4. Throne
5. Earth

Answers will vary. Students should justify their choices.